Gathering the Quiet

Gathering the Quiet

Thos. R. Hines

Contact the author at:
fridayletters48@gmail.com

Printed in the United States of America

First Printing, 2023

ISBN 9798376680438

Cover design by Kerry Hines LaCross

Interior design by Debora McNeer

Author photo by Jennifer Ragone Hines

Permission granted for use of logo by Kubota USA

In memory of
David W. Hatch
And
Edward J. Farrell

Table of Contents

Gathering the Quiet

I was born on Halloween 1948 in Ann Arbor, Michigan. In grade school I went to catechism in Quonset huts at St. Alexis in Willow Run, not far from the WWII Bomber Plant. The Sisters knew everything about God. One summer I had to memorize a mimeographed truth each day before I could go out and play baseball.

Later, with degrees in philosophy and theology, I earned my living in the construction industry.

In 2015, I wrote a note to several friends and sent it out on a Friday morning. One of them, Martha, wrote back saying it was a good Friday Rx for her. The readership grew and the practice continued on Fridays for the next three years.

In 2020, still not comfortable with the management of creation (so much 'noise') and still not satisfactorily 'knowing', I began writing and sending Friday Letters To God, predawn ponderings, calling, wondering, cajoling, trying to say what is unsayable. The response has been favorable.

Let's start with Friday Letters To God, gathering the Quiet.

Thos. R. Hines
Autumn 2022
Irish Hills, Michigan

*"People don't come to church
for preachments, of course,
but to daydream about God."*
                                    – Kurt Vonnegut

PART ONE
FRIDAY LETTERS TO GOD

I

WINTER EXPECTATION

Expectations

My brother writes
'You expect a lot from God'

I don't know what to expect
I don't know whether to pray for rain
or get off my ass and invent irrigation
Or just let it be

What if I run away and hide
ignoring sadness and turmoil
What if I cry out 'Lord Lord'

What if a happy dog licks my face
and I not take self so seriously
this cold winter morning

Reel

Dear God
What shall You do of me
still soft clay after many years
a Spirit dangling as if by cable
like a marionette, clop clop
on wooden floor
acting the fool
a well-intentioned hobo carrying
too large a backpack
Reel me in

Name

Dear God
Will you warm me in sun
Will you lend certitude

Another day, another cup
Another beggar at the off-ramp
Teach me to navigate the
prickery path
What is your name
Is it 'Yes'

Half-a-moon

Dear God
Is it okay to give you a call
this pre-dawn with
half-a-moon clear in the sky
Could you send sun to melt winter
and warm each bluebird egg
Melt me gently
to fertile soil

Bystander

Dear God

I, your guilty bystander, clueless,
entranced

Shall life be a moment of beauty

Or a stew of coming-to-be

Commandment

Dear God
Pre-dawn
Will light light the way soon enough
Will coffee make for optimism

What can be said that is true
Can word and symbol be trusted

Lend comfort to the afflicted
Walk humbly with God

Acorn

Dear God
Like a lost shoe
Where are you
Shall I ring bells and light candles
Sit in supplication
walk the dog
clean the bathroom

Maybe I should shrink into the
space of an acorn
into the place-less Heart of God

Stopper

Dear God
I rarely talk about you
(as if I knew what to say)
You're kind of a conversation stopper
who's leaked in since childhood
rattling around
finding place

You don't text
People dress You in silly clothes
I sit in quiet
Waiting, trying to be open

Squeaky

Dear God

Come into the moment

Cool overheated self

Wash away sweaty opinion and judgment

Spread Knowing as if from an oil can to our

squeaky hearts

as we wake from the sleep

of unknowing

Body

Dear God
This body
A wonderment
A mystery

Hover near
flow the juices
lend Joy and Gratitude
Bless our unknowing

Earth

Dear God

Go ahead, heal the earth

All this reckless consumption

I recall Mother Teresa in an interview

in Detroit in 1978

was asked what *should we do*

She replied that, first, we should pray that

Earth be not worse from our being here

Pinned

Dear God

Your realm so large

So many zip codes to manage

How will you find me

and keep me pinned to your jacket

like a flower at the eighth-grade dance

Monday

Dear God

Monday morning

I don't feel like talking

You okay with that?

You, standing by your holy ironing board

in an old bathrobe, cigarette dangling from lips

(Paint that on the chapel ceiling)

(I thought you were going to quit)

Okay, let's have coffee

But don't talk

just for a while

Truer

Dear God
On a winter morn
this pesky noisy self
like an unruly scratching puppy
Cute, but …

Empty me of me
Lend Truer Vessel

As If

Dear God
Amidst kaleidoscope of rattle
Come
Clear my sight

Guide these well-aged arms
(Only an eye's blink from
childhood sandbox)
Still digging, tossing sand, working
as if an ant or bee
As if

Wisp

Dear God

Let me hide in the folds of your skirt

Unable to invent satisfactory self

puzzle pieces imprecise

chain not fitting on sprocket

This 'me' invention, so fragile

Potter's clay wobbling on Your wheel

A touch please, a wee wisp

II
SPRING AWARENESS

Spile

Dear God
Your moon is a third now
Visible between slim branches
light at dawn
All that phloem and xylem
we learned about in tenth grade
How much shall I invent
and how much comes
from Truer Source
May we tap it like the maple tree
Wisdom drip-dripping from the spile
and then cook it down
renaming it 'Grace'

Shepherd

Dear God
Teach this marionette to dance
this wooden boy to be true
this restless child the way home
to the palm of your hand
into your vest pocket
onto the tip of your tongue

Language and symbol
to say what is not sayable
Each calls to God
in word and gesture unique
according to longings of heart

Send the slightest shepherd
a flower, a bee, a word
to lead us home

Melt

Dear God how is it
we assign you human features: arms, legs
rules, tyrannical behavior

Perhaps you are
'beyond' human assignment
Yet 'knowable'
like the sun at dawn-
far enough not to melt us
close enough to melt us

Ant

Dear God
A good day to walk Earth
treading gently
aware of bounty
not consuming
not disrupting

When we are little boys
a constant occupation
is to scuff ant hills, to mess
neatly formed sand mounds
Or better yet, to pee on them
There, a nice lake for you Mr. Ant

Now, an old guy
I refrain
from disrupting tiny nations

Bug

Dear God
What *are* we this morning
this you/me
Are we hotdog/mustard
distinct but co-mingling
Invisible surface tension
me a bug on your pond?

Pace

Tread gently in your wanderings
God sits in a tiny cart along the way
Turtle, up from wetlands
tows God-cart in warming sun
at a pace known only to Turtle and God

Blessed

Dear God

Blessed be the frozen dawn

Blessed awakening

Blessed the deer low in wetlands

Blessed be busy hands and sunlight

Surely our hearts will thaw

Surely we will rise and mix batter

This is the day the Lord has made

Let us rejoice and be glad

Sleeve

Dear God

May we be true with resources

Not greedy or wasteful

Let us not foul the air

Let us be healers

May we tread lightly

May You wear us on your sleeve

Seeds

Saturday dawn
Four deer slow-walk in lowlands
mere shadows blending in
mounds of sedge grass
past mid-February
Winter's back broken
Soon maple sap will flow

Dear God
May I write you a card
As you have written me
Word and sound
color and shape
touch and scent
seeds of spring

Spring

Dear God

Baby leaves of the big elm

chilly at first sun

The oak holding back

Sweet cherry readying to burst white flower

honeybee's delight

On the ground brave hepatica

like shy seventh graders up to dance

Violets quick to follow

Spring peepers

Turtles in the driveway

We enter Garden

where we cannot but uncinch

our hungry hungry Heart

Hold On

Dear God

On a snowy April day

Flowers wearing wintry shawls

Young leaves in chilly white teepees

Hold on

just a few hours

Let the sun butter your toast

Grow

Dear God
Shall we contemplate creation
Or play with goofy dog
Yes

Canopy outside forming, greening
readying to protect southern exposure
in heat of summer

Sometimes we walk in clover and orange flowers
Sometimes in mud

Be wakened
"Plants want to grow" (Edwin King)

Tree

Tree as art and beauty

Takes sun and makes shade

Takes waste and makes mass

Bares wings to God, smiles upon the sky

Anchors to earth, sipping and sharing with a
thousand tiny tongues

The home and future home of countless species

Each in turn, for a while

Nudge

Even if we are bathed in Light
Even if Bliss attaches for days
like a chigger bite,
still we walk dusty gravel,
deerflies relentless
Complete, yet somehow incomplete
Content but longing

Wild raspberries not so strong this year
But *here* at the edge of wetlands
an unexpected bush lush of blackberries
Tactile awareness like a pricking branch
The God of Humor nudges
again and again

III

BUILDING HOUSE
WITH GRANDSON

(Note: I'm building a house for son out front on an acre by the road. I suspect it will come up in these Friday letters.)

House

Dear God

Building a house

Rearranging dirt, what did you hide down there

undisturbed these eons

for me to hit with steel shovel

Sand and gravel from glacier

Am I building a house

or trying to be found

To Know and to be Known, to

lose separation

Nod

Dear God
Builder of houses
Can an old guy do it once more
Body and confidence shaky
Shoulders throb after one day
Actually, feels kinda good ...
Kiss-my-ass you aches and pains
God-in-a-nail-pouch
Let this house be *art*
Lend the slightest gesture
a nod in this direction
Strap it on

Foundation

Dear God

Sunny day

Frost-laws off

Giant concrete truck belching like a greedy dinosaur

Trench walls holding

to welcome tons

of slush soon solid

to carry the load

May the yoke be easy, the burden light

Ode to a Circular Saw

I've a house to build
Shall I order a new Skil Worm Drive,
Mine wore out after thirty years
She looks to most
large and cumbersome
an oversized locomotive, blade on the left
To those of us grown up with her,
she is machinery art
on the job of any knowing carpenter
or tool snob.   Yeah!

Slab

Dear God

Pouring floor slab in a couple hours

Grandson sleeping in loft

Dog stirring, coffee dripping

A good crew coming

Unforgiving concrete

always a risk it will misbehave

like a two-year-old at the grocery store

May old guy boots lift spritely

in heavy cement

like springtime fawns

one more time

(next day)

(five old men and a thirteen year old,
floor near perfect!)

Feast

Dear God

On Saturday morn

Successful work yesterday, body ache

Good ache

Grandson sleeps in loft

Dog rests at foot

Bride sips coffee at southern window

It needn't get better

Resting in the quiet Heart of God

Enough is a Feast

Build

If I forget Thee Lord let my tongue cleave to my palate

Work looms, a house to build

Wood finding place as walls and roof

stoutly connect to concrete base

Fenestration offering light and passage

Three-dimensional order from flat surface

separation of inside from outside

House takes shape, possibility of *home*

Stops By

The Oriole stops by for grape jelly
squawking loudly at the empty vessel
I up and spoon her a healthy dollop
Her song sweeter as
dog sidles up for morning love

Brother stops by from North Carolina
to help
We'll sheath the roof
20-ounce hammers and a worm drive saw
It will take a few sheets to regain
the rhythm we had fifty years ago
before OSB and nail guns

IV
BRIDE AND DOG

Smile of God

Dear God
On a Sunday dawn
Dog and bride asleep
She must have stayed up late
A pecan pie sits at stove top
mysterious art
And jars of maple syrup
lined in rows, sealed for storage
Each drop, drop, drop
gathered at tree
harvest of Gift
affirmation
merged with toil
and cooking-down
The crooked smile of God

Shoes and Dogs

Dear God

What is the greatest commandment

while drinking coffee

awaiting the dog and

bride to rise

Are we different after fifty years

Gone through a bunch of shoes and dogs

some houses

Still adjusting and cooking down

Trying to diminish pesky ego

The greatest commandment?

Try to be good

don't be a jerk

be generous

open heart vault

embrace all as One

Issues

Dear God
All these issues
Do I have enough cream for coffee
Does the dog stink
Should she be on the couch
Will the oak buds survive
Will the bee find pollen
Will you come around if I don't assign you a face
a name, a purpose

Are you
the place between artist's brush and paint
the quiet between raindrops
How can I *not be* of You

Glimpse

Dear God

Years ago my bride insisted I put a window

high on the south wall

Grumbling, I did so

How did she know You would put your large moon

there, above, to greet me early morning?

A window peeking into Heart, a glimpse of Light

as You whisper, *'Before you were in your mother's womb, I know you'*

Rest

Dear God

Mind spooling

Scrolling countless concerns

All this noise

Day of rest

A not unreasonable tradition

The dog, meditation walk, unhurried

Reach out

Allow kindness to fill the vessel

Joyfully

Dear God
Are you the Joy of wife and dog
chatting about breakfast,
abundantly accepting and endlessly forgiving
Are You like that
Accepting, forgiving

May wind be gentle
the sunrise warm
May Your smile find us
May kindness fill our hearts and heal wounds
May we dance Joyfully with wife and dog of morning

V
ALONG THE WAY

Bridge

Dear God

If I couldn't sleep

I'd get in the truck at 4:30 a.m.

and drive to the all-night restaurant

I'd write a letter to my mom in Florida

on a paper placemat

I'd send cash for her bridge tournament

She hasn't had mail in twenty years

The grimy eatery gone

Who will take my call in the uncertain hours

Minus 2

Dear God
Minus 2 at 7:00 a.m.
Do I need commas?
Do I need boots and gloves, an igloo
Do I need a project or better knees
What signals 'enough'

Shall I change jobs
Shall I sit at sidewalk in Paris, penniless
and drink bitter coffee and smoke bitter cigarettes,
borrow paint or clay from hungover friends

Chilly thoughts
        Signed, Crusty Old Guy

BookClub

Dear God
A weekend North
with BookClub, our thirty-fifth year
Six of us now
A lot of books and babies
Some heartache and loss
Still good energy and voice
generous sharing
amidst wine and beer-soaked interruptions
kindness and acceptance
unless you choose a stinker or
didn't read the book
At table, a wisp of prayer, a grand meal
We start earlier and end
when signaled by a member napping
on the floor
BookClub

Sprinter

It is not important that your granddaughter
win the race

What is important is that you wait in the windy
bleachers

while she huddles with her seventh-grade
teammates

She sees you, that smile, she waves

She runs

Her time in the 100-meter sprint

clearly under a minute

Woodchuck

I've been peeing each day into the woodchuck hole

under the ramp of the garden shed

Not a neighborly gesture

though less aggressive than trapping or shooting

We're not yet to where

the wolf shall dwell with the lamb

It's asparagus season, maybe the woodchuck
will move out

VI

GLIMPSES OF GOD

Mereness

Dear God
I've a life-long suspicion that You A*re*
that there is something *right* about You
that You self-reveal on your own schedule
and cherish the mereness of humanity

Knock

Dear God, why are some
pretty in middle-school, while others
amble around the edge of pain
in shoes from the cheap store
How come some feel good and some
are crushed
Do we make this up

Maybe we *choose* to participate
only to find the prize soft
'That's it?'

Later we return to the
basement-door-of-god
We knock
God whispers
Come in, Come in

Sit

Dear God, dare I seek you

Sun breaking

warming Sunday morn

Wanting to sit on the porch with you

What is Your desire

Only my heart?

All You want is to sit with me?

Wow! Sure

Sticks

Dear God
How is it that each morning
all existence is shaken
like a box of pick-up sticks
then re-strewn
in disorder

How about it, this messy pile
Can't You just take it away

When one tired mom or grandma
cares for a child
it profoundly reshapes All Creation

Lower Case

I don't mean to be disrespectful

by placing 'god' in lower case letters-

It's not a proper noun, like, say, Yahweh

I think god is not too concerned with grammar

I think god is very fond of me

and allows me to chew on her bathrobe
like a puppy

We assign god gender

and human qualities so

it is easier to understand

We prefer god convenient and available

to help find parking in Ann Arbor and

cure cancer

yet there is greater godness whose Name

is beyond our comprehension

There are many Paths to the Heart of the Beloved

We all get there

Sometimes

Sometimes we are angels
cinched to the hip of God

What if we are
inseparable Oneness-with-God
temporarily embodied
as if in tight fitting shoes
This life

Sometimes we are needy humans and
god takes us out for ice cream

Chapel

In the quiet of chapel

fifty years ago

A stone loft, old oak

lingering incense clinging to heights, enveloping

An image of Sacred

A Moment

May we find 'holy place' and 'holy moment'

Towardness

Dear God
I see a picket fence
a country cottage, gardens

Each day a step
subtle, as if 'towardness'
Small doses of bravery
Crack open the door
just a smidge
That we may be Light

Ineffability

Dear God

I come into You

uncluttered of symbol and language

Not of form but *awakeness*

unhurried

Staying awhile

where time is not

Shedding adjectives

bowing to ineffability

and Presence

Happiness

Happiness comes up my driveway
Unsure of her intention, I hide
as if she's pushing religion with
those pamphlets and a clean shirt
Risky business
I mask up and wrestle her to the ground
She touches my cheek like the kiss of a child
Helpless, I surrender

Thin

Dear God
Your Dwelling so near
Some partially enter
unsure, feeling, testing
Some bump it as if a steel curtain
as if driving a tank
God sighs

The veil between us and God
is thinner than truck-stop toilet paper

Theologizing

God so loves

and makes a unique universe for each of us

with its own 'rules', circumstances

and perspective

It is difficult to live in community

A blessing and a curse, it is said

Some contend their own universe is the 'right'
and 'only' way

Not helpful

Slow-walk among the forgiving purple flowers
on the forest floor

Shards

Threads of our fabric
tiny tick-tack-toe shapes
intertwined, layered
space between, big enough for
a logging truck
a teeny tiny truck, driven by a
teeny tiny driver on a tiny road
Unless there are no roads, then she will fly
on tiny wings, the bucked logs chained firmly
on the way to a sawmill beyond the star
Any star will do, a tiny one, not out there but
in here, deep, deep in heart, making heat,
sending light
enough
to light many worlds
Shards of God

VII
WISDOM, PRESENCE,
GRATITUDE

Imprinted

Dear God
The sun does not wait in its travel
regardless our intent
Time, the great tease
passes and we are imprinted
in ways we did not suppose
Only in retrospect do we see
Only in stillness do
we know

Wiggling

Dear God

I can't find you

Am I hiding?

Under the couch?

In the belly of a whale?

How far must I go to escape you?

'I will hound you all your days' You say

'How can I forget thee' You say

'For you are held, and tattooed

on the palm of My hand'

Quit wiggling

Be Held

Washed

Dear God
Why this restlessness
as if sitting on the nose
of an endless freight train
trying to peddle it as if a bicycle
trying to make it go

Who cares
Step off
Rest at edge of Shady Pool
Soak feet in Holy Water
Be Washed

Constantly

Let each do her job
As if orderliness abides
As if goodness a possibility

As if Song amidst discord
As if She whispers your name
Constantly, endlessly

Minus 3

Cold out, minus 3
Exhale
Be blessed with gratitude
for no reason
Un earned
Un bought

Featherlight
Neither body nor thought
Unencumbered
Lofted in Current
Loosed from tight fitting shoes
just for a while
Receive Gift
Be Gift

Day Begins

Sun trying to penetrate morning chill

I bet on sun

I bet the chicken crosses road

I bet the goat stands on picnic table

and leaves an offering

Day begins

What did you expect

Fresh donuts?

Get up!

Make something happen

Brother Ass

St. Francis of Assisi, when old and crippled referred
to his body as 'Brother Ass'

Some of us are experiencing 'oldness' of body
Bodies like a barn-find '57 Buick Roadmaster
Clunky, not sleek like young live-forever bodies
In need of repair, parts hard to come by
Yes, we do drone on about our sputtering engines
and wobbling joints
It's not as if we can step out and climb into a new F-150
Wouldn't want to

At best we dwell in Wonderment
the breeze of God, just enough to move our wind chime

Formless

Into the formless heart of hearts

The quiet placeless place

The reign without reign

Only Presence

Rest in God

Go often, be refreshed

Made anew

Shimmering

God sometimes enters like a sliver
An unexpected harsh intrusion
We probe the entry with
our clumsy pocketknife
The wound heals over
leaving remnants
which resurface
shimmering
throughout a lifetime

Happiness (part 2)

Happiness,

the sister of Gratitude,

like a summer fog on the wetlands

envelops

Available

like her brother Presence

Let her lay upon you

pricking those dense defenses

Quit swatting her as if a mosquito

Four Fragments

Before I made you in the womb, I know you.

Jeremiah

Get off your ass.   Make something happen.

C.E. Hines (my dad)

Two prayers – Help me. Help me. Help me. (and)
Thank you. Thank you. Thank you.

Anne Lamott

Yahweh asks only this, to act justly, to love tenderly
and to walk humbly with your God.

Micah

Letters to God

A rickety platform
A Kool-Aid stand
on sawhorses in the yard
Kool-Aid, 3 cents
Few passers by
Ice cubes near melted
Mom's sugar settling to bottom
A sweet venture
A path with heart
Good try

Enough for now dear friends, the basket near empty

My bride and I noted our fiftieth wedding
anniversary
yesterday, August 18, 2022
We went early for a bite at the tavern
Then walked to the ice cream place

Amidst the noise
May we Seek
May we be Sought
May we walk Kindly
Th

PART TWO
FRIDAY Rx

I
LONGING

Sadness

We all have a sadness

sometimes

sitting on us like an elephant

Even during sunshine

it catches up with us in all our pretty occupations

clinging to us like sand burrs

just for a while or sometimes longer

Relief

At the rest stop on the expressway

Great relief upon entering the men's room and
seeing a urinal

Not the usual relief

But verification I've not entered the lady's room.

Battery

We charge the battery of our phone

And the battery of the dump trailer

And the sun charges the battery of the golf cart

And the sun charges the battery of each tomato

We rest in sleep charging our own batteries

Eight hours. Beep, beep, full! Up and run.

Endless cycles like an ox at the water wheel

Do we know how foolish we are, sometimes

the ends we'll seek to hide from

That Which Is

(or whatever Her Current Name)

Lunch

We have a longing

to enter the inner place

without sound or gravity

or image or symbol

or expectation or measure

and quiet the soul

snipping away grasping tentacles

Into free fall

(or is it soaring)

Into the limitless mindless mind

this nourishment

a light lunch with God

Lawn

Waiting on the lawn
outside of heaven
Having a coffee
Not enough of the old energy to sally forth
Not giving up, just resting
Biding time, as they say
Just beyond the fence
goodness aplenty
Actually not too bad right here, on the grass
cool breeze, shade

Pouch

Little pieces of hurt
kept in a pouch
A troublesome wart in the pocket of life

Toss it in the air
like a tennis ball
Hit it like those TV tennis champs
Boink!
Past the moon
Shattered
into weightlessness

Driveway

Let me walk the driveway

And meet the morning sun

Let me be small –

Small enough to greet the gray green tree frog

Unhurried

chipmunks chattering

Wild berries at rest

What to make of the day?

Maybe step lightly

and leave it alone

Temple

Oh temple of the soul

blundering bumper of walls at night

attached for a lifetime

Brother Ass

stimulated by a mere five senses

a toothache for eighty years

this body a tight fitting pair of shoes

        Persevere

find a tiny lens

a cloudy eye into the heart of God

Ponder

It is prayer

to sit and ponder

reinventing creation each morning

while the dog laps water

from the toilet

and the radio drones an ache of continents far

    Stars clear in the sky

        a sharp slice of the moon

resting

        in the vest pocket of God

Out

Unable to welcome light
Heart propped with withering posts and
temporary signs of 'keep out'
Too dark

Beauty
cloaked in negativity
Hardly a chance for her,
or her sister,
Wisdom,
to make an appearance
Both like fragile eggs in the pocket of a dirty
apron
waiting patiently
for release
like seasoning sprinkled on creation

Whisper

Starved for a God moment-
just the slightest tickle
a miracle in a thimble
Whisper my name
Yeah, me, Your loyal lap dog
begging a morsel
Not my best Buddha self
needy and craving
      Make the day into night, move the
planets left and right
Make the tree frog hide in view
Any ol' thing will do
      I am here, just in case, here I am

Grace

Sometimes we live in the dark for so long
that we forget the light
Everyone's had moments of light
haven't they –
when Presence is close and overwhelming
and we want it to stay forever?
Some try to possess it
inventing handles
Some think it is
result of chemicals or spicy ethnic food
Some call it Grace
a piece of precious we cannot hold
and yet remains, as if in our cells

Morning Damp

Open the glass

Let in the morning damp

Birds tentative

Chipmunks with muddy boots

Air pressure expanding and contracting, ears popping

Each leaf dripping

Night water seeping between blades of grass

through loam as if making earth coffee

between stones and grains of sand deeper
and deeper into the aquifer

sifting, purifying

Each drop of water a tear from God

longing for home

Wind

Our cares and attachments
weigh us down and
change the gift of color from radiant to dull

We are seekers while young
Then householders
Perhaps the onset of wisdom finds us
while raking leaves in the wind
The laughing swirling wind
slave to no concern
unraveling our tidy plans

Flow

As if we could see – and paint life
as if with watercolors on flat canvas
A snapshot
foam on beer, condensation on frosty glass
a pretty maiden, flower in hair
a smile
a moment
one among many – add color and dimension
and time, forward and back
atoms and molecules
universes known and unknown
we begin to experience complexity
Is it ours to build further?
Or to be of heart in the moment we have?

II
ALONG THE WAY

Gift

The gift of existence – the beating heart we cuss
as over-subscribed, broken and put upon by the fates
For a morning minute
be still and mystified
soften mouth and jaw
push back fear
move into day
with kindness
and intention

Her Face

My brother took out money
for the person with the sign by the side of the road
Embarrassed, I wouldn't look in her face
She'd spend the money on … something

       She doesn't like being there, he tells me,
reaching across, forcing me the bill as the light
turns green
impatient drivers behind as I pass money
real human eyes burning for a moment
mine, hers, sparks of compassion, his
as we move on
window closed

Box Store Girl

Box store Corporate Miscreants
I've been wronged! Mislead!
I'll stew till my ears steam
I'll go back and yell at the girl

The one who got out of bed and fed her
three-year-old and
took her to her mom's and drove to work
in that old car
the one that needs brakes
to her paltry wage job and
her helpful silly vest with her name
She'll be waiting, calling me 'Sir'

I see her
slightly haggard, a notch shy of pretty, trying her best –
beautiful beyond comprehension
I can't be mean to her –
really, impossible

Old Fellows (circa 1995)

Implement at road side, for sale

Dad and I park the truck and walk up

I stand on the farmhouse porch as my aging father

bangs the door harder than necessary

An equally ancient man, roused from nap opens the door

glasses and hair askew, suspenders pulled over stained long johns

large belt buckle hanging loose

      The two stare, wordless

sizing each other as if old gun slingers

I step back, uncomfortable, slightly embarrassed

at this toothless encounter, this pending chesty negotiation

      Finally, my dad,

"What outfit you with?"

"Old China Marines. You?"

"Fleet Marines, detached"

I notice the old man's belt buckle emblem, and melt further away

as they each recite serial numbers and landings

from a lifetime ago in the Pacific of WWII

I was not part of this conversation

a fellowship beyond my comprehension

Jelly

Sticky jelly on the light switch – Grandchildren

Pleasant thoughts

Rapidly passing years

Innocence and wonder

A wash of color, a palate of infinite possibility

Rosy cheeks glisten like stars

As it should be

All of this

even though its likely my own jelly on the switch

Drummer

I see the drummer behind the band

He lost a young son

I wrote to him a note

Maybe as much for me

I know him only a little and now this other kinship

I explain how at the grocery store in the
fresh vegetable section

it finds you and

hits you in the chest, out of nowhere

stinging, taking your breath away

Let it wash over you, I tell him, don't hurry
or hide from it, let it run its course

than fold it like a handkerchief and set it aside

I don't remember exactly what I wrote

It might have been too invasive

I did not hear back

And now two years later after the park concert he
loads his drums

and walks in shadowy summer dusk

I greet him, Hey

He nods, Thanks for the note, he says

Raggedy

These must be the raggedy underwear she
mentioned

Shall I toss them now

or wear one last time?

If the garbage collector finds them, need they be
fresh and clean

or, if I get in a wreck today, the nurse at emergency

you know?

Shall I risk?

Pretty comfortable

I'll toss them after wearing

one last time

If I remember

St. Pat's Day in North Carolina

A blessing

May you eat spaghetti like a small child

May the meatball find you

May you walk sunny paths on quiet morns

May that awful fear come not to be

May your time at airports be short, your landings
soft

May the smile of children penetrate your soul

May your needs be few, your wants dissolve

May you fly, effortlessly, blissfully,

on magic carpet with the Beloved

even though most of the time you are sure it's
bullshit

May your day be mixed in the breath of God

For surely *that* you are

Holy Day

Fourth Wednesday of the month
government funds magically into my account
What to make of this
free money suddenly appearing
Almost embarrassing
Yes, I worked for it, made deposits, waited
I hear of those in need
but don't send the money back
keeping it instead in a little pile to buy gasoline or
take my wife to dinner
She still works at a job where she gets paid
I still work, too, at various jobs but don't get paid,
except by the government
Here, let me take a moment to check the
computerized direct deposit ...
Yup, there it is, like manna for the Israelites
Maybe I can buy something new and shiny, a bell
for my bike or new baskets
from Shaefer Hardware downtown, with the
squeaky wooden floors, where my dad took me in
the fifties.
If we were lucky, we'd enter the ancient elevator
and ascend by pulling a heavy rope
up to a secret haven full of dusty treasure
I wish we could go back there
the bell on my bicycle just not the same
'wing, wing'

Firewood

So much wood to split

and then to stack

in long neat piles two rows deep

loose enough for a mouse to run through

but not the cat chasing it

Piles covered to shed water and hold snow

sides exposed for drying

Long rows like bank accounts assuring winter
warmth

Ash and cherry, oak and hickory, a little elm and
hornbeam

each piece handled five times

finally settling among glowing coals

thoughtfully and efficiently

radiating warmth

More cumbersome than the snake-like quiet of
natural gas

Tactile

Makes you feel alive

And ready for a nap

Up North

Young boy holding a large turtle
in his lap like a cat
How *does* one snuggle with a reptile
Young boy with shovel and ax
digging and chopping
as if it makes a difference
(It does)
Young girl with a frog
large green and wet
nose to nose whispering
Children like a mob of fish
all in unison sprinting to a next adventure
At dusk flaming torches on sticks
crushed between graham crackers
with chocolate.
Ticks enough for a zombie movie
Ten children power washed and clean
Off to bed
Half an hour after me

Green Apples

Boy, about eight, sitting on the toilet after eating
green apples,

terrible stomachache

Same guy, 60 years later, waking four A.M.
identifying with, and *being* that little person, living
that moment, now

The old guy and the boy are the same- the *time*, as
we say, is the same, indistinguishable

I am the young boy and the old man right now,
housed in this flexible body suit

pretending to be lineal, stretched like bubble gum,
for a lifetime

With a certain orderliness

we act our age

the body suit no longer drawn to green wormy
apples.

Egg

Young girl

afraid of spiders, ticks, and

things creepy crawly

spots an egg in the dusky shadow of the hen house

Chickens clucking near, she

musters all her bravery and steps onto straw
and droppings

reaching

extending fully, she grasps a warm brown egg –
a jewel for her dad

She smiles

He smiles too

A fine victory

Barefoot Waterski

Almost light at almost six

Meet at the dock, expensive inboard,

Detroit V-8 sitting lustily center-boat, a throaty
rumble idling across glassy surface

Colorful suits, in the water now, bare feet, "Hit it!"
and the engine roar

Up and gliding at the end of a long rope

giant rooster tails from our heels at thirty-eight
miles per hour

glistening in the rising sun visible clear across the lake

not so long ago

pastime in past time

Away

San Juan Islands –
Like the chilly craggy coast of Scotland
and the sea goes on forever
while giant cedars and firs
stand like arrowheads
pointed at God

History compresses on vacation
Sounds and sights blend
As if in a mixing bowl
How are your legs today and feet
It's good to be away
In the swirl
And to go home

Grandchildren

Driving for grandchildren

8:15, pick them up

To the bakery, an apple fritter please

and to the tractor place, stop and

climb mighty land crawlers

Quarter mil a pop? No problem

I'll take four

Then home. Nana hugs. Dog hugs. Dig a carrot.

Climb a tree. Drive the cart.

Haul some wood. Swim the pond. Whoo!

Need a nap. Not yet noon. Day and a half to go.

Two days a week not needing to know or judge

Two days without the gnawing ache of managing
the universe

Juxtaposition

Dawn a drizzle, earth all green at rest

Modern robot in the kitchen noisily harvesting ice
cubes, readying for human consumption

An odd enterprise and juxtaposition:

the work of Mother Gaia and that of Brother Man

proud lime-green bathtubs and leisure suits

avocado wall panels in the family room

and prized stereo speakers,
large as washing machines

filled with woofers and tweeters

but none so glorious as the wren singing
out my window

in the shifting hazy green of morning's misty leaking
blue of sky and promise of day

Fall

Glass door closed, fall's first cool

Dog's toenails on hardwood

Wife prepares to teach

Festival soon, field mowing in earnest

Other work continues, harvesting, preparing for market

Always something needs the oil changed

My own oil is overdue

maybe a little STP would help the knees

Green leaves of the canopy at rest

waiting patiently for sun

Dust of the road not yet stirred

Oak

Giant grandfather oak vertically split, leaning
across the driveway

tired of holding on, weeping to the west

We took her down, safely

An old friend, a timber cutter

A slot here, a wedge there, the long-bar Stihl
fully plunged

A mighty crack, a moment of rush, thunder heard
half mile away

as the tree fell after countless decades

humbly, to lend warmth many cold nights

Timothy (2016)

"Hi Beautiful," he says, too loud, his arms spread, his silver hat-hair wild as he greets the hostess. She is beautiful and takes in stride his greeting as she leads us to a table. I'd picked my brother up at the group home to go to breakfast.

"That's not appropriate," I say.

"You're not my dad," he says.

She is indeed beautiful.

It pisses me off. He orders inefficiently, a la carte breakfast, this and that on the side, expensive tomato juice. "Order off the menu," I grumble. (Who drinks tomato juice?) He shares his side of bacon with me and offers sausage links for my dog.

He'd lost the debit card I got for him. The family joke was: His drug dealer doesn't take Visa. I couldn't give him cash. He'd bum money on the street. A guy gave him a hundred dollars couple days ago, five twenties. "How much you got left," I ask, sipping coffee, finishing breakfast. One twenty, four ones. I noticed he had change for the parking meter. "Where's the rest?" I ask. He gave twenty to such and such, a pack of smokes to so and so …

He was a crazy artist, a semi-street-person, giving away his art to coffee shop servers, generous to a fault, unaware, unfiltered, unconcerned with propriety. He saw the innocent wonder of the beautiful young woman at the restaurant and did not fail to celebrate that moment.

He was difficult.

He died a couple days later. Tipped over and died at the group home. "Drop me off here," he'd said, "by the bus station." "I love you," he said. "Okay, yeah," I said, "see you later."

I shake my head in wonder.

The Day

Perhaps today is the Day
when the sky opens- a crystal glow
and all accessories of earth
melt like Styrofoam battle tanks
arithmetic fails
time relents
And God reaches out His mighty arms
(He has arms today)
And He says to me Greetings, you in whom I delight
It occurs to me that God is rather formal
And He says Behold, Let's get outta here
And I am happy climbing deeper into Her mighty
kangaroo pouch of being

                  I'll give it till noon
If it doesn't happen
I'll drive to Kluck's in Ypsi
for chili dogs

Wonderful

Check messages

See if anyone says you are wonderful

Like eating popcorn or chewing gum –

we check the machine

Curious addiction

Can't we know we are wonderful?

Please:

you are perfection like a tasty tart apple-

wonderful!

Acorns

Acorns letting go like little skydivers
Plink plinking on the roof and deck
Little ball bearings of delight
Parachutes unopened
A one-way trip
to deer and squirrels in queue for feasting
    Like turtle eggs
some few hatch into new life
One acorn in a googol turns into a giant oak
arms spread like a mighty grandpa
connecting sky and earth

Career

When I had work for the men
they were happy
It was my part to get good work
non-adversarial
Do the job
collect the pay, move on
A good journey mostly
Always evolving
constant focus or get crushed
At some point get out of the way
You can't just stay out of habit, you get hit by a bus
and spill your purse in the street

Hummingbird

Hummingbird scolds as I pee off the porch

Her nectar near my ear this foggy morn

Who *is* the porch boss?

Each of us confused

going about our business

now retreating

thinking, reasoning,

to the extent that humans and bumblebee sized
birds think and reason

We could set a schedule of mutually agreed times
and needs

or

I could pee elsewhere

Grandma Gail

Grandma Gail died after a hundred years
I hear her voice and tone, enunciation and vocabulary
in her sons, delightfully so in Bill, the horseshoer
I'd asked son Bob if he'd given her permission to let go
He pondered the question as we sat by fire sipping beer
Son Woody plotted a family cemetery, it took a while
they're not a fast family
Maybe they were stalling and she knew it
Making her wait
At last complete, a pleasant location
in well-drained gravel
A fine place to rest
after all the heavy lifting

Side Altar

At my father's funeral I told the priest

he'd been angry at the Church for half-a-century

having to be married at the side altar

because he was Lutheran

My mother Catholic

in 1946

As if he were some kind of second-rate human

      Was he able to get past those feelings,
asked the priest

Sure, I said,

A couple days ago

Christmas 1952

Laying on my father's chest

squishing his pack of Camels

and wanting a bike for Christmas

A red one I said

as he lifted me in the air

suggesting a chocolate color bike

Chocolate would be fine, I agreed

which was the color of the

Huffy Convertible bicycle near the tree

the following morning

I must have just turned four

                  Oh, for each of us a fond memory

a complex father

like gravity tilting our being

Subscribe

We don't get to choose our neighbors

or the spouses of our children

We don't get to choose our parents or siblings

Unless we subscribe, as some do, to the notion that
we set this up in advance, prior to birth, our lifetime
a theatre of sorts where we play it out, go back,
trade roles and do it again, ten or a hundred times.
All this in an instant, simultaneously, a moment of
trial separation from God, frequently hellish, as
separation from love is.

Is that how it is?

Beats me

Kiss

Laying on the couch reading

Granddaughter, age 3, approaches

"Grandpa, I wanta kiss you"

I lean my cheek toward her and receive a glob
of sticky goo on my face

Back to reading

"Grandpa, I wanta kiss you"

Cheek extended a second time

"No Grandpa, I want a tissue!"

Rubbing

Tall oak, twelve inches in diameter, straight up

nine feet from where I sit

rubbing the house when the wind blows

It would have been easy to cut the oak prior
to building except

I don't cut living oak

Which shall I amend: The house or the oak?

Is there a middle ground

a non-destructive coexistence?

I'd hate to chop down my house

Perhaps if I stay out of it

the house and tree will co-mingle and

birth baby tree houses

Stone Wall

Who commissioned this work of art

This rambling curved stone wall that is our life

Tended by many hands

Shifting around trees and forest

Indirect at best

And weathered smooth

Moss covered here and there

Who said enough material exists

And so what if deer jump its height

And mice burrow below

Bacon

Early morning

Sitting at restaurant with grandson, age 4

Waitress brings each of us a plate

Pancakes, scrambled eggs, bacon

Grandson ignores his food, takes a piece of bacon from my plate and eats it

I sip coffee, watching.

He takes second piece of bacon from my plate, eats it

"What are you doing?" I ask

"Grandpa, I'm sharing with you."

Growing Pains

We can't dip our children in a pool of protection

as if in hot fudge or an industrial coating

They must paddle their own canoe

bumping rocks and getting sunburned

even though we warn them

too many times

We want seat belts and lead free paint

but kids have to be loosed or else

suffocate in a whitebread cocoon

They have to get skinned legs and risk poison ivy

if they are going eat lush berries near the path

Apologies to William

Shakespeare remains difficult
Out, damned spot!
Trips to Canada, the stage in England
Cliff's Notes and frustrated instructors
Sure, something's there but …

So much to grasp
neither can I play violin nor
drink good Bourbon without Coke
Each takes time and investment of heart

I prefer to amble a sunny edge of wetland
with grandchildren discovering blackberries
and wildflowers,
mushrooms the size of Narnia, and
green turtles big as John Deere tractors

Summer 1959

Oh, we could run forever in summer evening play

Tackle pom-pom, hide-and-seek

Impossibly thin bodies, dirty with ripped shirts

Unconcerned, unsupervised

All the fun we could have between supper and dark

Little kids too, allowed to join, teased, pushed down
and picked up –

everyone could play, the rules vague and fluid,
between sprints to bases-   a hut, a hole,
a chicken coop

till we came in and bathed the earth from our bodies

and soundly slept

Weld

In the shop welding a brush cutter

needed right away at the farm

Super-hot electricity melting steel together

Reinforced with additional metal

without having to mine the earth and experiment for

a thousand years

Thank you, old timers, for trials and failures

burned eyes, calloused fingers, hammers and anvils

that I might simply walk to the shop

flick a switch and meld molten metal hot like the sun

Disproportional, this bounty

Memorial

All these people

all those times

pictures, youthful carefree moments

pinned to the waving wall of a yard tent

and us, now, bending forward like old people

Campfire singeing the edge of ragged emotion

Junk emptied from the barn, a lifetime of worn stuff

ready for discard

loaded on a two-axle trailer by sons and beer-laden
buddies

Just bend over and do the work

sweat it out like a pesky cold

Later, exhausted by well-meant hugs see

children run carefree chasing a large ball

sunshine, the yard green and shaded as

healing flows into crevices and seeps in

Columbine

Columbine, the flower, tall and purple
sneaking outside the safety of large stones
at garden's edge
into crushed gravel and danger of driveway
How dare they?
Fragile beauty
moving at will
unbound by rules-
borders, territoriality

The children encircle with stones the curious
columbine,
rerouting large automobiles
protecting innocence, as children will

Carrot

First carrot of the year

with grandson

Like an orange Creamsicle

from childhood

only better

Or an Orange Crush

from the machine at the gas station

where your dad put in a dime and slid the bottle
along the chilly rack

once in a while

and now

this orange carrot, with wild green hair, at the farm
with grandson

Back Home

Fireflies gather at dusk

Welcome home tired Old Guy

Familiar driveway weaving between walnut and oak

around hill past two tree huts and the shop

grass sneaking between pieces of crushed granite

car swallowed by garage

Rabbits and chipmunks scurry from lurking
Driveway Cat

Darkness wraps and bundles Homestead as if a
package

to be sent into Night for rest and healing

then seized by Tomorrow

another Dawn

Going Back

Sister on her way to work
in morning dark
a first day back after her spouse died
Sitting here unable to assist her
Sending beams of encouragement
like the parent of a first day kindergartener
fragile like tinkling china cups
exposed to chilly winds
that seep through walls

High School Wrestling

Underwood the Hulk

was written on the picture

of a strongman taped to a home team locker

at the Christmas tournament in 1964

a two day event, the first for me

We second-string wrestlers wearing old uniforms
were entered along with the varsity

Locker rooms were quickly trashed and disgusting
after weigh-in

Still, no one dare rip down the menacing figure of
Underwood the Hulk

I spied him at his locker with his big chest and
Buddy Holly glasses

The following morning, we met in the semi-finals

It is not so much the match that I recall, as the hour
before, under the bleachers

frightened to a point of breathlessness, for the first
time unknowingly maneuvering into an altered
state

a hyper mindset, not to win (never really a
consideration) but, *not to chicken out,*

to be, somehow, *totally present*

Later, that evening, after our varsity guy wrestled
for third place, I lost in the championship match

not yet understanding the art of mental preparation –

a path I'd stumbled onto that morning under the
bleachers prior to soundly defeating

Underwood the Hulk

Brownies

Lunch table next door at the organic farm

A half dozen farmers and interns, bounteous fresh produce

I brought brownies

"Who made the brownies?" an intern asked

"A friend of mine," I said, "a peace activist"

"Oh," he said, reaching for the plate

A young woman, vegan, new to the group leaned forward

"She's a poet and teaches at prison," I said

The young woman's cheeks gained color

I paused, watching her focus intensify

"She went to Africa to hold sick babies," I said

The young woman's chair slid back as she reached across the table

"Maybe I'll try one of these," she said

Parts

Our father's work bench
A glass tray of parts
from a forgotten project
A film of dust and oil
Perhaps a carburetor or the motor of a machine
Brittle glasses from the dime store
Needle nose pliers, tiny screwdriver
What to do with memories
And jobs incomplete
Is lifetime ever complete
Does it reverberate, tiny tickling vibrations
ever here ever now

Travel

Early morning London

walking by a disheveled beggar

It's like driving by a vegetable stand on the highway –

you go by a few times

I should stop

after Starbucks where I'll spend

several British pounds on coffee

then study strange coins

while the ill-kempt blanket-clad street person exhales

cigarette smoke into frosty air

acting his part

waiting

as I drink expensive coffee

Buddy

My best buddy of eighth grade died recently
I was displeased with him-
his lack of restraint
taking the easy way instead of working
toward his boundless potential
He moved out of state
after retirement from the factory he hated
where he abused substances for decades
somehow avoiding dismissal
I didn't know that, late in life, he'd come clean
and helped others struggling with abuse
These later years
all my unnecessary judgments and displeasure

Voice

In the field where we played baseball every day
lay loose pipe end to end, each twenty feet long
A hundred of them
To be buried and change our childhood paradise
into a subdivision

Inside a pipe midfield I spied a one-inch ball-
bearing
halfway from either end
Being ten at the time, and alone, it seemed a good
idea to shimmy in
and retrieve the hidden gem
I got all the way to the ball-bearing before realizing
I was stuck
unable to go forward or back
Awareness and panic set in

Then a Voice, not my own child's voice, but mature adult-like, masculine as I recall,

comforting and with surety,

came from within me or from outside, I am not sure of where, but clearly voice

words instructing, "Relax. Back out."

Which, after making myself small, I did

I didn't think much of it at the time

An angel perhaps? Every night we said the prayer "Angel of God, my guardian dear,

to whom God's love commits me here ..."

And now, six decades later, with grandchildren that age, I have frightening flashbacks

and fear for them

And still gratitude and awe

for the Voice

New Glasses

I ordered new glasses

They arrived crooked

The salesperson studied my face

The receptionist behind the counter suggested

my ears were crooked –

the glasses were fine

I asked if maybe she had other things she could
focus on

She said, no really, we get crooked, especially
as we age

different parts of the body change size and move
around

I didn't ask for examples

but continued to view my slightly unbalanced ears –

brackets for vision hardware

I could better see both women

Nice smiles, pleasant, fairly balanced

Someone's Daughter

Chilly young woman

looking as if she slept on the street

inhales deeply on her cigarette

in early morning frosty air outside a coffee shop
in south Wales

Purple highlights in her hair, tattoos, bangles

Two more drags on the smoke

before dousing it on a patio table

Cautiously she enters the stylish coffee shop,
eyeing the busy baristas

and glides by to the tiny unisex restroom

After a while she reemerges, again looking toward
the workers

She exits the store

and relights her smoke

III

CALLING OUT GOD

Out of Order

The knocker on God's door must be out of order

Surely God would answer if only God knew my
concerns

I want to tattle on creation for being unfair

For taunting

The yoke oughtn't be loaded on those already
burdened

Open up!

I insist God send down little angelic load adjusters

　　　Surely righteousness prevails

but in the dark night it is difficult

at the edge of understanding

on the doorstep of God

Prayer

The childhood prayer
we learned from our mom –
Has its term expired
like the vaccination on our arm?
Is there a new prayer more hip and timely
fitting changing fashion
more inclusive
less fearful of spooky forces?
Shall we pray in colors and silence
in thunder, lightning and supplication
in song and dance
in the void without image
on easel with brush and bursting shapes?
      Any way at all will do
ask your mom

Embrace Goodness

I keep trying to figure

as if it's my job to manage creation
It never happens the way we think –
Perhaps life just goes on and we live it
Sometimes it works and sometimes we take lumps
   Still
I wait for the great burst of light –
the heroic resolution when
we rest unburdened in the arms of the Beloved
   Meantime
sit near moving water when you can
Embrace goodness
Release anger and hurt
Love a child and learn from her or him
Till soil
Welcome wildlife
Slow down
and at eventide engage the farthest star
as if it were in your lap
for surely it is

Forgiveness

Forgiveness
What if we acted the fool
and could wake in the morning
and erase it all?
Some would return to folly out of habit
or boredom
What if we could really forgive ourselves
and others?

        Could I forget thee?   Let tongue cleave
to palate should I forget thee
Like dribbling water wearing down stone
the call
Come back to me, come back to me

Holy Visit

I need a Visit –
just for a moment
to realign the pick-up-sticks
all jumbled
Could'ya stop by
Hound of Heaven
Any Name
The slightest sign always enough
Oh?
I need to be quiet and listen better, blah, blah, blah
Come on, just a little jolt, a mini fix
Humor me, your faithful compadre, blah, blah
Sunlight
Friends, clean socks
Sure, sure
Enough already?
Ok, tell you what, give you another chance
I'll be here
Look me up

Lifted

Little boys and girls
let out for the summer
trying on the illusion of separation
wearing costumes of individuality
Look at me!
I'm a clown! I'm a hero!
Yes, beautiful
though slightly dissatisfied

Lift us up! (we implore)
and sometimes
we are
Lifted

Early Morning Grouch

Squirrels and birds on the porch

Green in the canopy, wakeful moon of last night

Coffee trying to penetrate the grime, trying to locate
a pocket of hope

New dock sinking in the mud

Dozens of chipmunks scurrying in the yard, fearless,
as if I'm not the mightiest of beings

as if their little boroughs are satisfactory protection

I'll get a cat

Not likely

The day will get better

I'll brew another cup

And split some wood and mow the lawn

And take a nap

Is that enough

Is there a check-off list

Be righteous, walk humbly with God, mow the lawn

Help

Let me help you fix your flat
Here by the side of the road
Obvious need
Just want to help a little bit
Just today
Can't heal the earth, the sadness
All that sadness
makes you want to hide
makes you want to cry out
Lord, Lord

Sleepless on the Western Slopes

Chainsaws and dead men
Invasive plants and invasive people
We're all invasive
on some level

Tears come and clean the debris of heart
Which bubble up as bad dreams
Breaking up sleep

Chipping away at the steep surface of mountain side
Neither climbing up nor sliding down
Only chipping chipping away

Yard

Land outside

cleansed of frightening predators

Only pleasant beings allowed, blue birds and wrens

Insistent mosquitoes separated by window screens

Frightening bears, driven off along with other
indigenous dwellers

The corners clearly staked, except in the wetlands
where no one wants to walk

Ownership written down in convoluted descriptions

and stored at the township hall where old people
gather for mac and cheese

How come I get to have a little piece of Eden

sitting on the thin crust of a wiggling planet

in a warped solar system

in a spiraling universe

for this one blink of an eye

Woodchuck

Neither a vegetarian nor an excessive consumer of
meat,

I consider shooting the woodchucks who have
undermined the gardens

Rascally invaders

Is my garden and porch more important than their
livelihood?

Wars are fought on such matters

I was relieved to read that Ramakrishna slapped
mosquitos

or was it Gandhi?

Still, I am not sure of the enterprise

not wanting to further upset the spin of the planet

Megan and Jake

Day begins, a piece of clay to mold
Default to warm and safe and plenty

What to make of those adrift
bobbing in hopelessness
bald tires, heater broke
tools in disarray, no tools at all
no skills, not a clue
Get up! We say, Rise!

It goes deeper –
to the molecules of hurt

Maybe I'll go to dinner, or buy a new car – I'll
feel better

Or maybe, be a teacher
One who is kind, and teaches
patiently, with grace, over a lifetime

Omega, N.Y.

In the extended moment worthy disciplines combine

and unworthy ones slip away

The young woman with tattoos

scattered about her body like mosquito bites

perhaps in time the dots will connect

Her leap of faith so visual

Her mom worries,

"Why can't she just have babies,

after a big wedding, (which we can't afford) you
know what I mean"

It's risky, *living*. Maybe we oughtn't have come
breathing up from water

But since we have

we choose a path

not perfect at first

only gradually freeing of clutter –

toward a humbling scent, the very breath of God

Heroic Myth

Overwrought of heroic myth

Capes and glory

Youth permissioned to kill

Under the guise of service

Under a banner of nation, an unlimited ad campaign

and colorful swagger

young boys (and now girls) buy in

(less boring than community college)

But grown-ups?

We bring home a dead boy

and call him a hero, and say he sacrificed all

It never comes up, what a lie we told, that he bought into

All those cars lining the street at the funeral

It never comes up, that it wasn't such a good idea sending him away, techno-dressed, licensed to kill

Himself killed, by an equally beguiled youth

Paint

Takes a while for paint to dry
We put our fingers on the sky of dawn
mussing the colors –
we slip in bravely
flowing with intent
waiting for the moment-
Or – when the moment does not avail
inventing the moment
We are made in the image of God,
like God's shadow
or Her painted toenail

When We Were Younger

Those clothes we wore
That buckle on our shoes
Those songs we sung
Colors and concepts once clear
melted and blurred like a rained-on homecoming float
That smiling European Mary with child
the cool blue of her wrap
faded
      Seeds remain
the pendulum swings
new symbols emerge
some silly, some earnest
new coat-hooks upon which to hang
our yearning yearning hearts

Quandary

To be active in the world. Or to live in quiet seclusion

To be a worker at the crossroads. Or a silent holy person

To preach. Or whisper to a single soul

To know with certainty. Or to be often unsure

To have met Personal Savior. Or to Wait

To be about the work of God.   Or to wonder if much human activity misses the point.

To be right. Or to be kind

To fear and respect the mighty Godhead. Or have a good laugh with the Beloved

To list precepts and documents of faith. Or listen to the wren sing

To hold language and written word as static in meaning.   Or, In the beginning was Word and Word became flesh and dwelt among us

Tipping

Is there a tipping point –
the 'Big One'?
Has it to do with oil or water,
plate tectonics, government?
Is it likely to happen in our lifetime?
Will they say, Well, obviously
the signs were there

      Or

maybe –
a bluebird will fly into her rickety house
and a butterfly land on
an orange flower, and we will watch and
dissolve
into a pool of gratitude

Jump

We want good sounds and shiny objects

and smells and tastes to make us whole

I sit outdoors and the wren settles my heart

Am I able to have the same sensation sitting near
the city dump in a nation of poverty?

Not likely

The dump, the wren and the green of the canopy
are temporary and illusive

Pointers and symbols of mind seeking oneness with
that which remains in shadow just beyond everyday
comprehension

What is it like to 'jump out of our skin'
just for a moment

And see with clarity

Some

Some among us walk in shadow
as if in quicksand
as if in excess gravity, in pain
    And some among us step lively
naturally gifted, unaware
of those beaten down
    The gifted ones
who seem blessed
but are without compassion
carry a millstone

            of unknowing

Better

Feeling gloriously better after illness

The urge rises to proclaim gratitude to the deity

Thank you! Thank you

for this absence of misery, this healing

only days ago incapacitated

   Yet – shall we lend equal responsibility
to the deity for illness?

It wasn't as if I got sloppy drunk and crashed in the
gutter – I was innocent

this time

If we praise the good, shall we curse misfortune?

An old question

Bearded philosophers and theologians over
millennia proclaim definitive answers

usually a bit wordy, while

I remain uncertain

yet filled of gratitude

Stick

A single crooked limb sticking up from the lawn

as if fallen from a larger tree

yet slightly alive and growing

Braced with a steel stake

bare and ugly all winter then suddenly

flowering, beautifully lushly bountifully filled
beyond capacity

this same spindly stick

Can something be both beautiful and not beautiful?

Is beauty a fleeting moment?

Shall we cherish its brevity

shall we embrace and breathe in this sneeze of God?

When

When is the time to be whole
To set stuff aside
and *be*
We wait for seasons
and jobs to complete
for trinkets and fool's gold

Could we be a Zen short-order cook
with a paper hat
Could we become unimportant
and charitable
a chance meeting
a tiny needle piercing a heart of stone

Body

I'm about done with this body, said Uncle Bill
shortly before he died
What if our body is like 'a cold'
something we 'get' and then 'get over'?

What if God is not anthropomorphic –
not a 'He' and does not have arms?
You gonna be okay with that?

What if we are –
formless
yet, somehow there is
caring and *knowing*
of each blade of grass and the chirping of the
smallest bird?

Altar

Early morning dark
in stillness waiting
A red glass hummingbird feeder
gathers light just before dawn
standing in for the ever-lit red candle
near the altar of a musky cathedral
The light is on
I see you

The Trek

I screw up so many times
I'd be lost without forgiveness
Is Forgiveness a 'stuff', like chocolate?

I don't think God keeps score
Keeping score is a human activity –
adding to the misery we insist on

Steer away from vexatious persons –
you don't change poison ivy by rubbing it
Still, respect its existence

It is not our job to be miserable
tread lightly, move on

Why

Why do some get to work at the hardware store
while others fall off the end of the world
Why do some have happy babies while others
suffer
Why do some have no idea at all
while others see clearly
Why do some struggle while
others are good at stuff

We don't get to know all there is to know
except in tiny sparks of understanding
once in a while
Tiny sparks that strip away our preposterousness
and leave us awestruck

Lauds and Vespers

'Help me Lord, Help me Lord'

Not a prayer, though said morning and night

not intentionally, but habitually, as if stepping onto
a high wire

a humbling awareness

the delicacy of moment

the folly of presumed control

as if the ground is actually solid

Maybe it is a prayer

Tossed

The wind blows
Let me hook my lanyard to Your robe
and be tossed about –
needless
refreshed

Thank You for this life –
this one snowflake
this single brush stroke

IV
WIFE

Tea Cup

I almost put toenail clippings in my wife's tea cup

She wasn't home and was done with it

I would have dumped it and put it in the dishwasher

It was too cold to clip my toes out on the porch

the cup was there –

Yet –

Two score back

she was such a darling girl in college

It just didn't seem like the thing to do

She's still darling

Most of the time

Orphans by the Sink

I like it when she takes a green leaf

broken by the dog, and plants it

new, in a small jar at the window

and it grows into a plant

Little orphans by the sink, decades of them

And she will dance around the house

with a watering pot, at the oddest time, her coat on,
leaving for work

upstairs downstairs her route of plants

Orchids and those flowers, blooming

whichever season

Who's to tell them different

Slip Off

If I slip off first

you may not want to stay here

All the maintenance, overhangs to paint, high as an
eagle's nest

We're not rooted like oaks and hickories

If I'm gone, you may not want to clear the driveway

or bring in the wood

I just say it, getting it over with, the saying part

Then again, it might be fine, who needs paint

You can work the gardens

and have the kids out

And call the birds by name

and the dog, whatever name

and the shop, empty of me

Give Billy the machine, he'll plow the drive

Oops! Here I am again reinventing your life
in my image

Together

Time together

Grumbling and rumbling

Like five year olds, my turn, my turn

Topics territorial jurisdictional fictional

Visitors arriving in a few days

She, diligent

Me, less enthused

about bedding or

trips to Ikea

I'll buy beer, perhaps liquor

Maker's Mark is it?

She'll get fruit, way too much, spilling over into the
basement fridge,

Hey, wait, who moved my beer …

The silly things we do, and say

While paddling this canoe, together

Be

Wife reading a flier from the mail-
Special deals, dreams fulfilled!
                    I stare at blank page
a crossword puzzle without clue or structure
Or perhaps
one clue only:
Be
                    Draw a little stream and some sunshine
A dog if you like and a child
and that house
the one with the crooked chimney
Hold the child's hand
Go from there

Autumn Morning

Cool sunless morning
  canopy of leaves still
Wife blanketed for autumn warmth
  content with cup of tea and readings
  the glass door open just a bit
  wind chime, its pendulum moving slightly
as acorns plink the deck
Now a soft dong of the chime
  a whispered reminder to waken further-
to bend time and light with intention
        Give us a minute
One more cup of tea
One more breath of quiet

Wednesday

Wednesday

I woke in panic

thinking I forgot and missed remembrance of the day Sammy died

As if the day slipped by without acknowledgement

I no longer dread the date's approach

but witness it, stare at it as if a mighty freight train, but from a distance, an observer

I did not miss the date, a few days hence, the 19th, confirmed with wife, breaching the topic

Next Monday. Perhaps I'll take a ride, escape to ... where?

Shall I call his brother? Or J? I don't know.

The first few years I tiptoed around the day, sidestepping, holding breath until it went away

Now I have gratitude, a day of remembrance, a celebration of heart, more like Easter than Good Friday. I don't know why.

This life, this illusive slip and swirl of time, this merest instant of form before exhalation to formlessness yes ... Yes.

Famousness

If I were famous

people would try to get ahold of me

at 2:00 p.m. as I contemplate a nap

I would have to respond, since the person bothering
me would also be famous

You have to respond to famous people

I have enough trouble responding to people I love

let alone bothersome famous acquaintances

So, thankfully I sit alone on Sunday enjoying the rain

not even the dog begging supper

I am fairly famous to my wife but she doesn't bother
me during nap time

Anniversary 45

An album of Simon and Garfunkel
A candle
A poster for the wall, things
I could buy for you, uncomplicated
money scarce and
wet shoes in the winter
didn't stop me from trekking to your door
wherever it was, at your school, your dorm
And you'd drive to see me, too far
in too worn a car, too late at night, for coffee
and an hour
That youthful blush
Just to see your face

Nesting

New flower garden along the sloped edge of the shop

All that work, border stones gathered and placed

and now it's cold and still bulbs to be planted

Yet she persists, 'amending soil'

amending my perception

inviting order and beauty

where I used to throw sawdust in the weeds

Communication

Many years ago our son got off the bus from
kindergarten with an upset stomach

As we greeted him my wife felt the waist of his pants –

These are so tight it must hurt

I just bought new pants, can you be growing that
fast? Let's get these off

Beneath his pants he had on four pair of underwear

We asked, Why do you have on four underwear

He replied, You said to put on clean ones every day

V
ON WRITING

Poems

Writing poems

Sending them down a smooth slot as if from a
gumball machine

many colors and flavors

hitting the end of the trough and popping out
on to the floor

Once in a while there is a good line or pair of words

or a twinkle from the farthest star

Once in a while it seems to work

Bread

I want to write a poem

and send it out right away

like fresh baked bread

still warm, to a friend or several

It smells so good, and butter will melt so nicely

But mostly it is better to wait and let it cool,

lest I offend someone

with these thoughts- they are thoughts after all

not fresh bread. Symbols and images pointing futilely

unable to say what is intended, feverish brush
strokes on what cannot be painted

So if the bread is sometimes not so grand, set it on
the porch for the mice

That would be okay, a feast of sorts

Spilled Soup

A poem sat
leaking off the page like spilled soup
Ingredients bumping noisily
symbols unable to meld
so wanting to point with meaning
to tell great truths

Little pieces of gravel in the road, what words are
sometimes locking perfectly into place, puzzle
pieces of creation
Sometimes flying in the air cracking our windshield
when
hearts become thick and dense like giant stones

(No offence to giant stones
whose hearts are like springtime flowers
purple and white, breaking through a blanket of oak
leaves
painting the forest floor with new and fragrant
sweetness)

Words and Meaning

Words come

like slippery logs

down a watery sluice

into a foamy pond

floating like marshmallows on warm cocoa

      Then again

sometimes words have to be pried out

like rusty nails

and put in proper order

      And later

words take on new meaning

so how can we hope to convey?

Yet they come

new words at dawn

like marsh gas seeping under the door saying as
best they can until they become new Babel heaping
up at the base of the tower until the tower is no
more and once again children romp and play atop
the crumbling battlements of former meaning

Of One

An audience of one
suits me fine
        If only
you could hear sounds
sent shimmering
scooped with clumsy spoon
stirred like mud pies and dried in the sun
sent for you alone this moment this day
reminding you
of the beauty that you are

Veil

Have a sip of tea

Look at words

See if they catch you

for a moment on your busy waking morn

Always a veil,

like mosquito cloth

separating us from what is most telling

A ghost of meaning

ever present

just out of reach

January

Winter cold
Words like boulders
dense and graceless
trying to penetrate molasses heart
Rain in January melting dirty snow
into plentiful mud

Suddenly
new snow at dawn, pure, straight down
an inch blanket
insulating the fur of deer
resting in straw lined pockets of wetlands
each a cozy nest in the hand of Creation

15 February

Dear Readers of Friday Rx,

I've been sick this week with a winter cold and have not been able to properly prepare a Friday Rx. Hope to be back in the saddle next week. Thanks for your loyal readership. Th

Morning Quiet

As if in a warm pool

and words are wet and melt into many shapes

then formlessness

    Meaning begins to massage body

and body is part of meaning and word

    Space between molecules vast

and worlds and ages drive through the large spaces
as if on a mighty expressway

    Then birds chirp and the dog wants breakfast

    and we reassemble new

    Again and again

Veni Creator

Come, teach words

Send imagery

upside-down, inside-out

opposites connecting effortlessly

making something out of nothing and nothing out
of something

shedding and shredding muddled armor

fresh and new

ineffable

That!

Yes, please

send That

Awareness

There is a moment from time to time

when the window is open and words fly in like
musical notes

We are not warned of their coming but must be
vigilant

like a woman making bread

sensors ready for good news

a whispered warmth

to be plucked from the weedy garden of today

and placed fragrantly in an open jar

for those who chance to stop by

VI

AWARENESS

Desiderata

Six pair of mallards glide on the pond

  invisible propulsion

    glass-like water, a sunny spring day

Just the slightest miracle

Spring peepers chat in the wetlands

Garlic greens peek out of winter mulch

Cardboard sign at roadside

  large dripping words running sideways

    youthful lettering: DOG FOUND

The fifth grade band honks through Old MacDonald
then

  impossibly

    performs

      Ode To Joy

If we do not weep in gratitude, we are not paying
attention

Lost

Sometimes we stop paying attention and get lost
We miss
little successes
    little flashes of light
        little pieces of redemption
that break the toil of journey
    We have to look, maybe strike the flint
Sometimes we make it happen, sometimes it just happens

Loss

When we lose a loved one to death

it is neither good nor bad –

it *Is*

Circumstances and timeliness may be weighty

yet

anger and blame

is not in the long run healthy

If we embrace a loving God (by whatever name and precept)

it is unlikely this God picks off loved ones as sport

    There is presumption in attachment

a clawing self-imposed burden

(indifference too is burden)

    We don't get to know all there is to know

    We best find a middle way, like the young Siddhartha

    Or like Mary Oliver, we must love with our whole being

and we must release

Beams

To be honest
and breathe what the universe has
whispered on raindrops and beams of light
Ever changing, ever constant
Gentle as a glacier
melting holy water
dawning daily
sweet fragrance of creation
smiling that quixotic smile
   Strap on boots, wash face
saddle up, hold on
or let go

Towardness

Rising from dark night

clutter of mind

Old fights refought foolishness

Waken!

In quiet, send out good intention

Though, surely

one cannot make a pot of soup with good intention

Start somewhere

a simple prayer

a *towardness* of heart

a whispered 'yes'

From the bed or chair with its indentation of your
round ass

stir all of creation

get on with the *Work*

Granddaughter on Her Second Birthday

In the months after her fathers death, I had a near-panic need to explain to my granddaughter (not yet two) that which is unexplainable. I wrote pages and pages, as if to keep her (and self) from falling off the precipice. Later I realized I was trying to gather what (I thought)her father would tell her over a lifetime. The following lines are a distillation of those pages, completed for her second birthday.

Delaney Jane

On the whole, it is best not to be miserable.

It is best not to lend misery to others.

Kindness is good.

If you cannot love, act as if you love.   Love may follow.

Negativity is a habit,

        a poor choice leading down the worm hole of lesser gods.

Be positive even when you are breathed on by fear and doubt.

Peddle your bicycle bravely through the minefield of community.

Do not be fooled by fashion.

If you choose to believe,

believe that you are loved and embraced

        beyond your ability to comprehend.

Clippings

As much as a fingernail clipping

is how much we know

living our obvious life, and

what if it's not really that way – time, density, vibration,

the urgency of it all

life as a concoction of changing imagery

Every so often a bump in the road loosens the bindings of illusion

Cables

The bonds we hold
Cables across a foggy crevasse
Cables thick and stout
enough to carry a full gondola
of smiling tourists
to the other side of emptiness
I miss my son this morning
just once in a while

A coming trip with little sons and daughters
remembers him

Goodness and lastingness –
are they really real
or made up
just for a while?

It's okay
typing black squiggles on a white plane
to soothe the burn of giant cable
squeezing my heart
once in a while.

Trees

Stopping in wonderment while walking the woods

Don't have to do all that *work stuff*

Really don't care to go back

Let younger men move the pianos

or go off to war as they insist on doing

much to the sad exhalation of wordless trees

each blessing us

forgiving our youthful stupidity, our elder hubris

ever forgiving

Attend

Shall we meditate while the dog begs for breakfast
Or while a child cries
A child is always crying

To what shall we attend
Shall we do great things
or weed the garden
A season for all they say
Good ol' they

For many, dimness lingers
compassion rises slowly and is dispersed slightly
as if from a salt shaker

Until
a shadow of awareness
a breath of kindness
working at this
our walk with the Beloved.

Compost

Hillside and trees swallow an old waterslide along
U.S. 12

So also the earth will swallow us

Meanwhile

let us not be miserable

Let us embrace the good

Let us be the good

Let us look past the folly of judgment

for surely we've not adequate information

Let us pet dogs and spit-clean a just picked carrot

Let us love unrestrained

Surely the earth will swallow us

All that insistence, just not so important

compost, good compost

Moment

Once in a while

dust and sediment settle

vision clears

noise abates

and we are with ourselves

be-lone, in the enormity of it all

unafraid, in the massive womb of creation

content, as if we've set aside this troublesome project

for a moment

Communion

Table

Clean off the table

Make a new day

Dive through the waterfalls

leaving old garments behind

Shameless

the wren sings while dropping waste

What will you choose, the song

or the droppings?

Some

Some harvest tiny pockets of gold
daily, confident that treasure abounds
Some feel locked in a room without direction
or social grace
Some have beauty
subject to time and gravity
Some are spectators only
Hopefully we are more than crickets under the
lawnmower
or rude lawnmower drivers
hopefully we steer around orange wildflowers and
the occasional foraging mouse

Toll

Pointless to hurry the honey bee
Or rush the butterfly from milkweed
Or coax an oak to walk
Lend time her toll
Her constant shimmering genius
Her mischievous promptings
Her relentless mirage –
A fresh cut flower in your hair
Fleeting beauty
Beauty indeed

Fortune

Calamity stalks the morning calm
Fortune though remains
lining her nest
with light and sound
and feathers
shed on a bed of oak leaves
Layers of life
guarded by a lone insistent bird
piercing dawn
like a lighthouse beam
"I am home, I am home"

Before

Before you were in
your mother's womb I know you
I am the tricycle you ride
the air you breathe
and the song before music
I am the shifting wave of every atom
the density of mass
and cool drink on parched sand
I am with you always
I am who am and cherish you

Falls Away

Blindness falls away

like pieces of broken crockery

over time

allowing vision into a pool

and we feel ourselves drawn to the pool, and immerse

and we are *of it*, and separation disappears

At first glance the pool is small and inviting

We want a taste

As we approach we realize the pool is enormous, and all consuming

We retreat many times

It's okay

No hurry

Clinkers

Like clinkers beneath a fire grate
stuff shakes out of us
a bit at a time

Enlightenment, Resurrection,
Awakening

Not frequently realized
A lot of tributaries to explore
We all get there eventually
Many paths

Traps

We invent traps
while laying in bed
then jump into them
'This is terrible' we say
'all this stuckness'
Why stay at that made-up place?
A short visit is plenty
Invent better
Leave stinky garments in a heap
Come!

Inertia

Inertia.

'Get off yer ass,'

my dad would say

'Make something happen

even if it's wrong' (that is, even if it fails)

      Start. Somewhere. Anywhere.

Letting Go

Lightning bug in a jar
Cannot last long
Lid removed
Let him go
Trail shimmering sparks
all the way to forever
Sprinkling sprinkling still
on us behind
        Quit of you Time
and you Space
capricious jailers both

Current

A *current* as in sea or sky
but without water or mass
A mighty flow of *empty*
that we enter as if a cloudy mist and
realize an overwhelming *presence*
           Dwell there
mindfully
needless
                And later go off to work
allowing it to flake
on those you meet
Invisible dots of joy

Illusion

Why are some socially adept and others clueless?
A flair of hair, a shape of hip, a curve of smile
all the difference makes
if we subscribe to that world
which we do, mostly
We stack our bricks and drink our portion of wine
       Then again, it is said
what you see – *what you think you see*
is not really how it is –
you are not this body
        You are Love
             and Loved

Form and Formless

It is said God is formless and
also in form
    and is in every breath and cell and action
      and is needless of these
        Every physicality is symbol pointing –
existing as expression

temporary, trying to reach that which is embedded
in memory

The memory too is symbol, trying to say what is
unsayable

trying to loose the loneliness of separation

Before (Exodus and Jeremiah)

Before I formed you

I know you

I am the air you breathe

and the song before music

I am the shifting wave of every atom

and cool drink on parched sand

I am that I am

and with you always

Staying

A compilation of moments
and stutter steps
Ordinary presence
A spot of compassion

Occasionally tiny bursts of light, hints
of direction, whispers of possibility
like tiny cups of coffee
at a sidewalk café in Paris or Havana

Staying for the long haul, weeding
this ever-demanding garden, discovering only then
purpose and understanding

Grace

When one stumbles in the dark

then sees the outline of a wall

is that goodness or merely dawn?

Perhaps goodness follows us always

and it is up to us to be aware

It is a small matter, but

if we take care of small matters

perhaps the large will fall into place

Let us not be miserable

Let us seek light

Let us *be* light

Positing Faith

My mother was Catholic
My father Lutheran
It seemed normal, though a little odd

Raised Catholic, I was formed
and informed on Thursdays by nuns
in post-WWII Quonset huts, schooled in the faith:
seven of these, five of those, several mysteries, etc.
At home we memorized countless mimeographed truths,
one per day, before we could go out and play baseball

I don't know the difference between what was taught
at Emanual Lutheran down on River Street and what we learned
at St. Alexis out in Willow Run Village

If there is Sin (big S)
it is the pronouncement and embracement of separation
We/they, us/them –
a smallness of mind and heart
an ancient mean-spirited blaming of 'other'

Grandson on Lap

Young grandson on lap

in the dark six A.M.

a quiet gift

As if the Three Wise Men have deposited their load

A brief moment

where all that matters is present

And then he is gone, like a firefly

to the bedroom, under the covers, giggling, cold feet
on Nana

Each

Each person is
a crossword puzzle without clue or structure
multi-dimensional
silent yet humming
salty yet bland
pliable
formable and formless, as needed
For each individual a universe created
for each is cherished that much

Acknowledgements

I am thankful to the readers of the original weekly Friday Letters To God for thoughtful notes in response, helping me understand what I was trying to say.

Thanks to BookClub (Martha Daniels, Tom Daniels, Eileen Hatch, Judy Wenzel, Sandy Hines) for decades and decades of discussing and encouraging the written word.

Thanks to Christine Ehrenberg, friend and reader several states away who led me to Debora McNeer, who graciously offered to take on the challenge of making emails and loose pages into book form. Wow.

Thanks to Kerry LaCross for cover art, just stick figures, I said, a five-minute sketch.

Thanks to friend and neighbor Catherine King, faithful Wednesday Editor, whose constant vigilance keeps me looking less foolish.

Thanks to son Luke, a constant Light.

And to my bride, sitting near in the quiet dawn.

Made in the USA
Las Vegas, NV
12 December 2023

82524531R00155